CALL AND RESPONSE

CALL AND RESPONSE

Sonnets by Rachel Spence

ILLUSTRATIONS BY
EMMA DAI'AN WRIGHT

For Sue, Jack and Michael

☙

THE EMMA PRESS

First published in the UK in 2020 by the Emma Press Ltd

Text © Rachel Spence 2020
Illustrations © Emma Dai'an Wright 2020
Edited by Richard O'Brien

ISBN 978-1-912915-48-4

A CIP catalogue record of this book
is available from the British Library.

The Emma Press
theemmapress.com
hello@theemmapress.com
Jewellery Quarter, Birmingham, UK

Supported using public funding by
ARTS COUNCIL
ENGLAND

CONTENTS

Prequel

Call and Response

Sequel

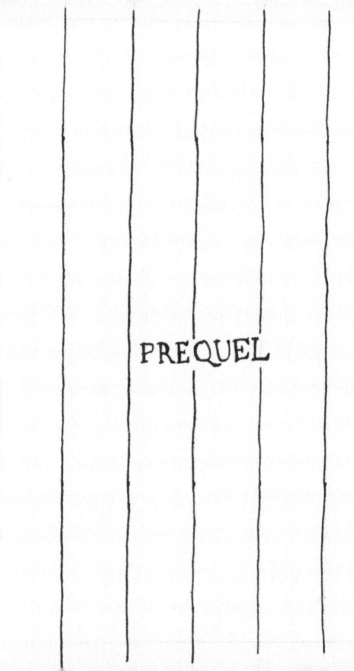

PREQUEL

July 1976, your garden, midnightish.
Our worlds distilled to nothing save each other
and this bewildering heat. I hear you
padding down the stairs – morphine trickle
of a mother's footsteps – beg you to let me
stay while you find whisky, deckchairs.
The lawn is dry as a ship's biscuit, but we are
watered by the scent of your tobacco plants.
My winter's bone is being old enough to know
I don't know what you're thinking. Not even
when the owls come. Two, maybe three,
their beatless wings spellbound against
earth's pull. Ten seconds we'll remember
all our lives. We know it, even then.

July 1976, your garden, midnightish.
Our worlds distilled to nothing save each other
and this bewildering heat. I hear you
padding down the stairs – morphine trickle
of a mother's footsteps – beg you to let me
stay while you find whisky, deckchairs.
The lawn is dry as a ship's biscuit, but we are
watered by the scent of your tobacco plants.
My winter's bone is being old enough to know
I don't know what you're thinking. Not even
when the owls come. Two, maybe three,
their beatless wings spellbound against
earth's pull. Ten seconds we'll remember
all our lives. We know it, even then.

July 1986, noonish. Our car's conked out
in the sun-cooked dip of a rollercoaster
B road en route to Ascot races. Punctured
or overheated, two hours from AA rescue,
your grin mocking the gods of tyres
and fanbelts. *We'll treat ourselves to lunch*,
you purr, in the posh restaurant on the hill.
I don't remember anything we ate
in that shady, foxglove-speckled garden
but I recall the friction of my pencil skirt
as I trudged behind you on the verge,
your dancer's calves powering up the slope,
shoulder blades jutting through damp silk.
The way your hips spelled smile.

October 2005, Venice. Six weeks after he left me
and *you're* the one who's grieving?
Excuse me while I slam the phone down.
I have pain to knead and other mothers to find
– the lagoon with her cloak of asters, the auntly moon.
You've smashed our covenant (I helped a bit)
to teach me one last lesson. The eight-year-old
begging a note to be excused from chapel.
We're Jewish, aren't we? Your atheism deep as tubas.
Don't come to me. Fight your own battles.
Instead, I learn the grammar of surrender.
Love, literature, my mother tongue – all lay down
arms at the first whiff of blood. And yet
my heart beats on. Just as you knew it would.

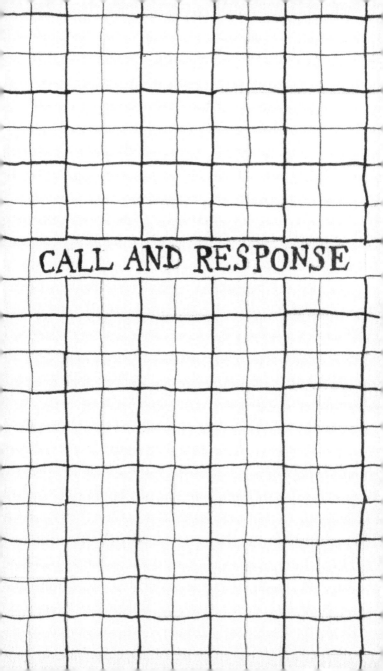

CALL AND RESPONSE

January 2013.
Commercial Street. Traffic fumes cauterising
the day to twilight. I'm between a broken
boiler and a visa application for a country
I can't afford to visit. Your voice like stale
water dammed too long. *You didn't come
for Christmas and now the neighbours think
we are estranged.* I'm done, Mum, really, done.
My phone sliding into the ninth circle
of misunderstood daughters. The queue
for visas Bablyonian – so many different faces.
All with mothers! And once again you're
buzzing at my hip. *Darling, how's your boiler?*
And once again, we're on.

March. My lover's kiss has framed my day
with light. Spring's diligent percussion
greening the tree outside my window.
The words flow freely, stitching me
into the morning's warp and weft. I've never
told you, have I, that sometimes when I write
it feels like letting blood. What haven't you
told me? What have we never asked?
Not now, Mum. But your voice is different.
Old-lady fear fluttering like a baby bird's.
You waited how long before going to a doctor?
Lay not that flattering unction to your soul
that not your madness but my trespass speaks.
The day no longer numinous. But we're still on.

April. The relief of finding you perched
on your hospital bed. Lipsticked and cashmered.
Defiantly undimmed. Twelve hours post-op,
you've drunk them out of tea and think you'd like
to go now. Nurses calling you the Steve Redgrave
of patients. Your healing seeded centuries
ago, tough as the ash trees fighting
their way through frost-bitten Polish soil,
hunger for a better life incubating
in clogged, shtetl light. And yes, I'm proud to be
your daughter. We've cared what the neighbours
thought since we were in the caves. My ancestral
grannies counted grapefruit spoons, possessed
small dishes shaped like avocados.

May. Your farmhouse huddled in Shropshire's
benign folds. I'm scrambling eggs as dawn
smears sherbet pink across the kitchen window.
It's strange with you upstairs. The dogs as well.
I drag them down to pee. The only whines
that you'll allow. I can't believe it's me
you want here. Though only you could ferret
my name out of a sacred text. *Jacob waited
seven years for Rachel and I waited seven years
for you.* (You've rejigged history all our lives.)
I'm terrified I'll hurt you when I change
your dressing but I am blushing
not at your scarred and holy absence
but at the way my hands are shaking.

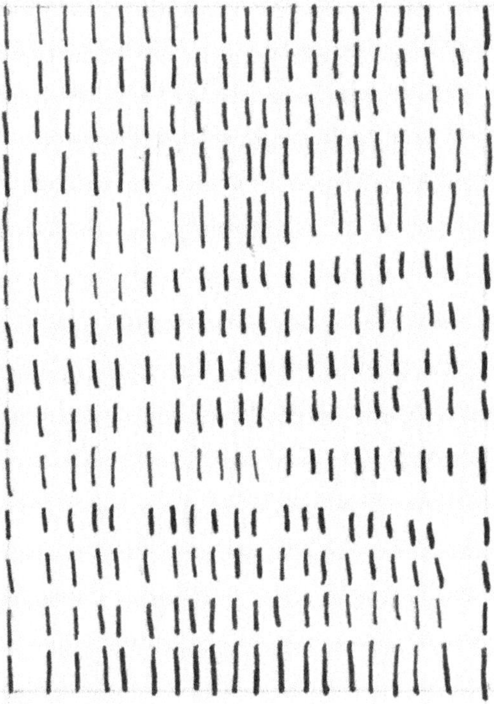

May. St John's Hill, Battersea. The guarded
heat of summer rain like 'sorry' on my skin.
Your call arriving while I'm en route to
the computer medic. You're done with doctors
and can we go to Paris? My skinny latte pooling
on the pavement. Omertà between mother
and daughter spilling its secrets into the cracks.
You'd tell all too but I have never tortured
you like this. Passengers on a bus watching me
as I have watched crazed people melting down
on London streets. The rain falls harder.
I want to smash my laptop on the road.
Female Moses railing at Her Lady.
You can keep your fucking tablets!

May. Still. My fifth espresso and it's not
yet ten. The silence between us scored
by a master builder. Notes of concrete.
Chords of blood and feathers. Noir edition
of those days when two of us together in a room
meant one of us was struggling to breathe.
Nothing has prepared us for this place.
Though I remember nights driving through
the cowled Welsh dark, your fairytales braiding
us tighter, tighter... The way we both hate spring –
its sharp, green birth pangs heralding so very little.
My father's name staining the screen like milk.
Will I accompany you to your surgeon?
And once again, we're on.

June. The doctor could be my younger sister.
Let's throw jealousy into our toxic mix.
A childless writer in my forties, nothing I do
matters very much. But briefly, in this room,
I am a good daughter. You're the Scorpio
but she and I have trapped you in our pincer
movement. My dad's the poker player but we
are gambling like pros. She's bid you chemo-
therapy and you've called our bluff with zero
treatment. We'll call it quits at six weeks' radio –
I'll come down on my birthday. We drink to it
at Morrisons' caff – tea the colour of a rubbish
perm and carcinogenic doughnuts.
Outside it's summer. Your garden waits for us.

My birthday weekend. You're wag-tail happy
as I shamble in. Your kitchen's far too tidy.
Where is the unswept cottage light? Who washed
the cat hairs off the cushions? Put ceanothus
on the table? Madonna-blue, whispering
that mother love is its own call and response.
The garden stirs and twitches like a river
pressing at its banks. Roses and hollyhocks
grown coltish with neglect. Your dream of controlled
wildness slipping into jungle night sweats.
You're making tea, denying soreness, sadness,
the shame of unknown fingers. *Move here. No, here.*
Good. Nearly done. But the dogs are quiet.
My father does not speak the whole weekend.

Your final check-up. August. Nimbus clouds
prised open by Delft blue. Waiting is hard.
The women serving tea and biscuits wear
survivors' smiles. This time we do not say
how young they are. How they could be me.
I know that I've inherited some of your genes.
I drink industrial quantities of tea. Feel naked
without lipstick. But what of your stoic heart?
Your gift for loving men? That blowtorch smile?
They're calling us. The doc says we can bugger off.
Come back in two years' time.
We'd rather cut off our own hands than cry.
Let's celebrate at Morrisons.

Lay off the doughnuts, Mum.

SEQUEL

7:01 am, May 2018. Your garden. Sun clotting
in the branches of a neighbour's maple, leaves
so dense the air around them cannot breathe,
beams sieved slowly as a mother's skirt sifts
the tears of her martyred son, the cloth pressed
to her cheek years after it has dried. I'm drinking
coffee, reading, writing poems, weaving myself
into a world where everything is still as it
should be: this beaten copper light, the clink
of china from the kitchen as my father makes
the tea he'll take up to your bedroom, a ceremony
that's lasted sixty years. No kimono needed.
I cleave to caffeine, love and words. Time blinks.
And once again, we three triangulate.

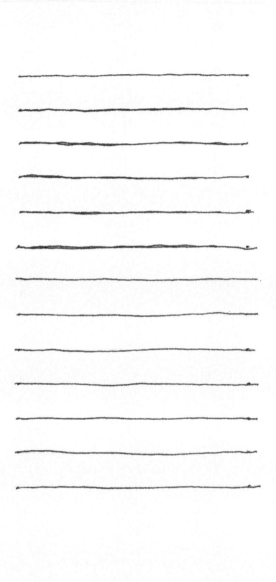

ACKNOWLEDGEMENTS

My thanks go to my mother Sue, for a lifetime of love, giggles and inspiration; to my father Jack for being the bedrock of wisdom and kindness on which we all rest; to Michael for sharing everything – and then a bit more; to Sofia Karim without whose light my world would be a dimmer place; to Nan McElroy, whose amazing heart gives me space to write in more ways than one; to Emi Takahashi Tull who continues to show me the way; and to Mimi Khalvati, without whose Versification course I could not have written these sonnets.

NOTES

The lines 'Lay not your flattering unction... my trespass speaks' is a rewording of the same line from *Hamlet*.

ABOUT THE POET

Rachel Spence is a poet. Now living in London, she spent nearly ten years in Venice, Italy. She has a pamphlet, *Furies* (2016), and a collection, *Bird of Sorrow* (2018), both published by Templar Poetry. Her poetry has appeared in publications including *PN Review*, the *Financial Times*, *Envoi*, *The Indian Quarterly*, *The Frogmore Papers*, *South Bank Poetry* and *Iota*. Her poem 'Antonello's Song II' was included in *The Forward Book of Poetry 2019*. In her day job she is a freelance arts writer, chiefly for the *Financial Times*.

ABOUT THE ILLUSTRATOR

Emma Dai'an Wright is a British-Chinese-Vietnamese publisher and illustrator based in Birmingham, UK. She worked in ebook production at Orion Publishing Group before leaving in 2012 to set up the Emma Press with the support of the Prince's Trust.

THE EMMA PRESS

small press, big dreams

The Emma Press is an independent publisher dedicated
to producing beautiful, thought-provoking books.
It was founded in 2012 by Emma Dai'an Wright in
Winnersh, UK, and is now based in Birmingham.

The Emma Press publishes themed poetry anthologies,
single-author poetry and fiction chapbooks and books
for children, with a growing list of translations. It was
awarded funding from Arts Council England in 2020
through the Elevate programme, for diverse-led arts
organisations to build resilience.

The Emma Press has been shortlisted for the Michael
Marks Award for Poetry Pamphlet Publishers in 2014,
2015, 2016 and 2018, winning in 2016.

The Emma Press is passionate about publishing
literature which is welcoming and accessible. Sign up
to the Emma Press newsletter to hear about upcoming
events, publications and calls for submissions.

theemmapress.com

Ingram Content Group UK Ltd.
Milton Keynes UK
UKHW050307100523
421472UK00010B/114

9 781912 915484